DROPKICK*romance*

DROPKICK *romance*

cyrus parker

Andrews McMeel
PUBLISHING®

for amanda

my queen, my heroine.

foreword

at the time you're reading this, cyrus & i will have been married mere months. in my own poetry collection, *the princess saves herself in this one*, i unfold the story of the abuse i endured as a child & how i managed to survive it. it doesn't sound like the typical love story—probably because it isn't. if anything, it's a self-love story, but i couldn't have written such a complex story without including my now-husband.

in *princess*, i wrote:

> he
> did not
> teach me
> how
> to love
> myself,
> but he
> was
> the bridge
> that
> helped me
> get
>
>   here.

- i thank the universe every day for you.

self-love is not an easy thing to achieve. it is often a treacherous journey you must make on your own. yes, i'm the princess who saved herself, but it was the bond i shared with cyrus that gave me the courage to approach the mouth of that bridge to self-love when it finally came after more than twenty years of suffering from silent trauma. when he let my hand go so i could take that long walk across, he waded rivers & climbed mountains to meet me again on the other side.

in these pages you'll finally be able to catch a glimpse of the wonderful man who helped me so tremendously on my way from victim to survivor. the robert browning to my elizabeth barrett browning.

you will also find the tale of two relationships. the first, a toxic & dishonest one that lasted too many years. the second, a respectful & fulfilling one that will, with any luck, last a long & happy lifetime. i have read & collaborated with cyrus on these pieces many times over the past year. rest assured: he is so talented a weaver of words that when he aches, you will ache. when he falls, you will fall. if i didn't already know the woman in the second half of this book was me, i undoubtedly would have fallen for myself.

proceed with caution. i promise you will become entranced by the likely all-too-familiar words of love & heartache you're about to read.

- *amanda lovelace*

i'm lacing my boots
with my words and
dropkicking the world,
because my feet have been
planted on the ground
for far too long.

— *DROPKICKpoet.*

i've always taken to
admiring people
from afar.

i never dared get close,
because looking back at me
was never hope—
the possibility of finding happiness
in another,
or someone finding their happiness
in me—

but instead,
the looming shadow
of rejection,
its sinister voice telling me
you're not good enough,
you'll never be good enough,

why would you think
you could ever be
good enough?

— *i never thought i was; i just hoped.*

too many people
have pushed me away
without ever giving me
a chance.

too many friends
have turned their backs
without ever giving me
an explanation.

— connectivity issues.

the thing about keeping
the world
at arm's length
is that it becomes

far too easy
to become attached
to the first person who shows you
the slightest bit of affection.

— *unsuspecting.*

we have the entire world
at our fingertips,
so why should we limit ourselves
to only what's around us?

— a web of hopeless romantics.

i was young and naive,
a heart filled with ideas
of what love
could be.

i don't know if it was
happenstance or fate,

but there we were,

polar   opposites

    drawn   together

on an earth-shattering

collision course.

— *brace yourself.*

where i was shy,
you were bold.
where i lacked courage,
you were fearless.
where i lacked experience,
you had more than enough
for the both of us.

— i hoped you'd rub off on me.

when words
are the only interaction
you have with someone,

you have no choice
but to get to know them
for what's on the inside.

— how is this any less real?

i kept my
trust under
lock and key,
guarding it like my
best-kept secret.

— and there you were with a set of picks in hand.

you were

a l l – c o n s u m i n g

every spare

        thought,

every stray

        word,

every single

        second

of my day

        was yours.

— *my one thing.*

i knew you had demons
you were struggling to
keep at bay,
so i swore i'd stand by your side
as you waged this war,
until the day
there were no more demons
left for us to face.

— *your demons are my demons.*

three
initials.
carved into the inside
of my eyelids.

three
initials.
burned in the back
of my mind.

three
initials.
etched into the very core
of my soul.

three.
initials.
like bullets in the chamber
of a pistol.

— *i'm just waiting for you to pull the trigger.*

just a friend.
just a friend.
just a friend.
just a friend.
just a friend.
just a friend.
just a friend.
just a friend.
just a friend.
just a friend.
just a friend.

— who are you trying to convince?

every single word
an excuse
without a single letter
of honesty.

every suspicion
a confirmation
without a single admission
of guilt.

— *fool me once.*

before
we got back together
you told me
that he wrote songs for you.

so i bought a guitar.
i thought that
if i could write you songs
like he did,

maybe,
you wouldn't
                                        leave
me
again.

i tried first
to teach myself
how to play
your favorite songs,

but i couldn't make my fingers work right.

the guitar and i
were not a good match,
so i gave up trying,
and i gave it away.

— *some things aren't meant to be.*

we'll wipe the slate clean,
tear out the last chapter,
start over from page one.

we'll pretend
none of this
ever happened.

we'll pretend
you regret
what you did.

we'll pretend
that i am not
damaged goods.

— *let's pretend.*

everything started
feeling
n e w
again,

like the first time
your words
made home
in my heart;

before those
three
~~initials~~bullets
made home
in my skull.

before i began
second-guessing
everything
around me.

— *before i began second-guessing myself.*

he drifted toward us
like a swirling black cloud
on a calm april afternoon—

i felt a storm coming
but you told me it would pass,
so i bit my tongue

as you ran toward
the wreckage
he left in his wake,

and when you came back
drenched in deceit,
i was there with a towel in hand.

— fool me twice.

how
many
times
can someone
make themselves
f o r g e t ... ?

— *i've lost count.*

even when you
put me first,
it still feels like
coming in second.

— *i'm tired of being the runner-up in my own life.*

the question
i should be asking
isn't *how*,
but *why*.

why does it seem like we're stuck on repeat?
why do i always feel like i'm never good enough?
why do you keep sticking the knife into the same wound
over and over again?

— *why do i keep letting you?*

you've sacrificed
so many pieces
of me,
it's only fair
that you sacrifice
something
for me.

— *i'm not asking for much.*

suspicion
held my tongue hostage,
crushing it
in its sandpaper grip
until i quenched its
thirst for knowledge.

i dug through the mud
until i struck water
and it pulled me under,
filling my lungs
until my chest
burned with realization.

i ripped myself from the water's
grasp and heaved myself
onto your front doorstep,
where on your welcome mat
i threw up all the truth
that i had no choice but to swallow.

— *and somehow drowning was my fault.*

you told me
your demons were a thing of the past.
you told me
there was nothing left to haunt us.
you told me this,
all the while turning around
and embracing them
with open arms.

— your demons are still my demons.

your self-destruction
wasn't something
i could stand by and watch,
even at a distance.

i've watched people i love
suffer endlessly
until the only thing left for them to do
was *die*,

and although i was being
every bit as selfish
as i was selfless,

i wanted you
to want this for yourself,
not for me,
because i knew

you were worth it
and i needed you
to know
that too.

— *i'm not giving up on you.*

i think i became
addicted
to the pain.
i knew
you were bad for me,
but i couldn't make myself

                              say *no.*

you took over
my every
waking moment.
i knew it wasn't healthy
and i knew it was getting worse
but i couldn't make myself

                              say *no.*

— *i'm not even sure an intervention can save me.*

left alone
on the cold tile
of an unfamiliar place
in a pool of my own tears.

— *my punishment for not trusting you.*

you knew i hadn't yet
learned to swim,
yet you took my hand

and walked me
into the deep end
time after time.

i don't know if
you thought watching me go under
would teach me how to stay afloat,

but it was because of you
i learned never to leave home
without a life jacket again.

— *it's sink or swim, and i refuse to drown.*

you ran into his arms
and held on for a
       split second

too long.
i didn't know him
and i didn't *need*

to know him
to know that
       something

wasn't
right.

— *i am not right.*

who is he?

       how do you know him?

    do you two talk a lot?

            hang out a lot?

          have you told him about me?

why haven't you told him about me?

— *how do i make it stop?*

"promise?"

— *how to trick yourself into coping with trust issues.*

a single word
treated like gospel,
an oath,
a spell,

that would bind you
to the words
that fell too loosely
from your lips.

if i couldn't believe
in you,
at least i could believe
in it.

— *i can't move forward if i'm always looking back.*

this isn't
the person
i
want
to be.

this isn't
the person
i
was supposed
to be.

— take me back to before i cracked.

i didn't question
whether
i had just grown used to the hurt.
or whether
you finally decided that i was worth it.

and i didn't question
whether
you had simply gotten better at lying,
or whether
i had stopped being able to tell.

i didn't question
anything.
i just accepted
this peace
for what it was.

— *if you can't handle the answer, it's best not to
   ask the question.*

the road between us
was fractured beyond repair,
but we refused to let it
crumble away into dust,
so we tarred up the cracks
and hoped it would
be enough.

— *the wound closed, but the bleeding didn't stop.*

it was now or never:
defeat the distance,
or let it defeat us.

— *i won't go down without a fight.*

six hours.
three hundred and fifty-six miles.
two hearts.
one love.

— *i-75.*

your walls were a work of art.
your entire life
mapped out in
sharpie scribbles
from floor to ceiling.

when you immortalized
me on those walls
all my doubts
were wiped away
and once again

i had hope.

— *sometimes, it's the little things.*

we walked aimlessly around
the grocery store
down the street
from your house

where you took me to
the complimentary coffee stand.
everything was still
as we each poured ourselves a cup.

i was never much of a coffee drinker,
so even though my cup
was more sugar and cream
than coffee

it was still
so hard
to choke down
that bitter taste.

— *i still drank every drop.*

we both knew
the distance
would be difficult.

we managed
to defeat it once,
but finishing it off for good

was the challenge
neither of us
could quite figure out.

— *but a challenge we were willing to accept.*

our last night together
filled with our hopes for the future,
premature goodbye tears,
and one final photograph

to remember what it felt like
to have each other,
however briefly
it might have been.

— *goodbye, for now.*

you'd think there would be
some sort of lesson here
in how quickly a good thing
can be taken away,
but distance did not
make our hearts
grow fonder;
it simply brought us back
to the exact same chapter
we left off at
before.

— *a false hope.*

i spent my time
wrestling the weekends away,
waiting to feel that
magic again
but in the process,
i discovered self-worth
and self-confidence.
i am more
than just
a relationship status.
i am more
than i had ever
given myself
credit for.
i am more
than this.

— i am mine before i am yours.

your nicotine-laced kisses
were no longer enough for me.

— *a cheek turned.*

there was
nothing i wanted more
than to turn our

d   r   e   a   m

into

r   e   a   l   i   t   y ,

but i couldn't
justify
giving up

e   v   e   r   y   t   h   i   n   g

for

o   n   e   t   h   i   n   g

when i've already
given you
every other piece
of myself.

— *my escape.*

so we'd wait it out.

we'd wait until the planets
aligned,

we'd wait until the sun
went out,

we'd wait until the earth's
dying days

to see if there was a future for us
after all.

— if it was meant to be, the wait would be worth it.

we had all the time
we needed

to lay the foundation
of our future,

but the bricks
crumbled
                    a
                         w
                              a
                                   y

at the weight of our touch
because they lacked

the one component
they needed

to   stay
w h o l e.

— *what is time without effort?*

you spent the entire summer in my basement
folding multicolored squares into the shapes
of cranes and puffy little stars.
it was endearing, i have to admit,
to watch you meticulously
make each fold,
constructing something so intricate
from something so simple.

but it's so sad, isn't it?

to know that no matter how much time
you put into creating something beautiful,
it takes only a moment
to break it back down, fold by fold;
to squeeze each star between your fingertips
until its light flickers and dies;
to pick each crane up by its wings
and pull them apart until

the tension becomes too much.

— *and it tears in two.*

you tried,
but you didn't try
hard enough.
i can't fault you
when i wasn't willing
to sacrifice the same,

but i'd hoped that this
would finally be the time
you'd put in enough
of yourself
to balance out
this buckling scale.

— *equivalent exchange.*

we spent seven years
traversing highways
in buses and cars,
closing miles by the hundreds—
sometimes meeting halfway,
sometimes going all the way—
to prove all this pain
was worth it.
from handfuls of days
to entire summers,
we tried to prove
that distance
was beatable.
we won battles,
but i don't think
either one of us
truly believed
we could win
this war.

— *sometimes, trying isn't enough.*

true love can conquer anything.
true love can conquer anything.
true love can conquer anything.
true love can conquer anything.

— but what if this isn't really true love?

i remember
cherry limeade chillers
and wandering around
the sculpture park
until the sun
began to sink
into the horizon.

i remember
sitting on the frame
of what looked like a sailboat,
talking, laughing,
enjoying the comfortable quiet,
and thinking to myself
that this is the moment

i'd always been searching for.

— *too little, too late.*

life is made up of a series of moments,
but a single flash of light
in a sea of darkness
isn't enough
to save our souls.

— *still, i held on.*

phone calls became
fewer and further between.
text messages went
longer without a response.

too much time wasted dwelling
on what you might be doing
wondering what i might have done
to warrant being left in the dark.

— *the dark hadn't frightened me until now.*

you were not
the first person i texted
when i woke up this morning.

— *pocket-sized rebellion.*

time

was the rope
in a game of tug-of-war
between a dog and its master—

i sunk my teeth in
and took however much
you were willing to give

but you
were all too eager
to let go entirely.

— *the pendulum is swinging slower and slower.*

you wore a mask
to hide your
true face
from me.

i wore a mask
to hide your
handiwork
from everyone else.

— *i'm not sure whose was more convincing.*

i could stand in the middle
of an arena filled
with people chanting my name
and it still wouldn't fill
this gaping hole
you left in my heart.

— but the show must go on.

you turned me into
the one thing
i had fought so hard
not to be—

it was my honesty,
my integrity,
that i had taken most
pride in.

but because of the need
to protect you, the need
to ensure that not a single soul
looked down on you for the things
you did to me

you
made a liar
out of me.

— it's time i come clean.

i'd begged and pleaded
for this one thing
and it was
the one thing
you couldn't give me.

— *honesty.*

he kissed you,
and you did nothing.
i told you to spend time with him,
and you did.

let's not pretend, anymore,
that this is working.
let's not pretend, anymore,
that you care.

— we both knew this was coming.

we decided to give it
one last chance

to see if there was
anything left to save,

to make believe
one last time

that we weren't
broken beyond repair,

and to write
one final chapter.

our ending,
on our terms.

— *i stopped short of calling it a eulogy.*

you said
you hadn't yet
made up your mind,
but i knew that was a lie.
i knew before we agreed to this.
i knew before i stepped on that bus.
i knew before i walked through your door.
before i asked you if you knew,
i knew.

— i always knew.

i don't know where i am
or how i got here.
it's like i'm watching someone else's
life from the outside.

everything seems so familiar
but nothing feels right.
you seem so familiar
but you don't feel right.

— *how can there be so much distance when*
   we're so close?

we collapsed into each other,
one big mess of tears.

— *this is it.*

i gave you my best.

— *that's all i had to give.*

a dog is loyal to its owner
without question.
it will protect them
against any threat,

will give love
unconditionally
and grant forgiveness
automatically,

for that is the nature
of a dog—they never
see the bad in someone,

and that is why
i stayed. that is why
i let you kick me in the ribs
over and
over and
over, until

you finally got bored,
tied me to the post
outside the greyhound station,
and left me in the winter cold.

— *nothing more than a stray.*

with one last kiss,
you whispered:
"this will not be
the last time
we see each other."

i nodded,
knowing that this
would be the
very last lie
you'd ever tell me.

— i'd make sure of it.

i tried to hide it,
to hold in the tears,
steady my breathing,
think about anything*anything* else,
but i knew
that every single person
in this overstuffed bus
could see the moment
my heart shattered
into millions
of tiny
little
p i e c e s .

— and i didn't have the strength to pick them back up.

the room was a blinding white
unnaturally bright
the kind of light
that still burns your eyes
even when you shut them tight
and bury them in your palms.
i turned away
from the other lost souls
as if they were the sun
and i icarus.
the ceiling
the walls
the floor
everything a blinding white
unnaturally bright
why is there so much *light*
when everything else
is so *dark*?

— *it burns.*

they say ohio
is for people like us,
but as i sit here
alone
on a layover in cincinnati
drowning in tears
and choking on irony,
i can tell you that ohio
is not for people like us,
after all,
but a graveyard
where people go
to bury their hearts
when love dies.

— i laid my naïveté to rest right beside it.

your name popped up on the caller i.d.
and at first i thought it was
a mistake, a dream,
a nightmare.

i didn't understand,
couldn't understand
why you thought your voice
is what i needed to hear

but what confused me most
was right before you hung up,
you told me
you loved me.

yesterday, i would've believed you
but i'm not who i was then.
somehow, in these few short hours,
i've become someone entirely different,

and through these
cloudy new eyes,
i now see
everything i didn't then.

— *this was over long ago.*

"where are you headed?"
the woman in front of me asked
as we stood in line,
waiting to move on
to our next destination.

it was the smallest of gestures,
but it's one that will never leave me.
she didn't know my story,
why i was here,
or where i was coming from,

but she cared enough
to ignore my swollen eyes
and tear-stained cheeks;
she cared enough to wonder
where this bleeding heart was going.

we might have been two
namelessfaceless strangers,
two ships passing in the night,
but she showed me a kindness that i
was all but ready to give up on.

— *if you read this, thank you.*

i woke up,
face planted against
the bus window,
crusty-eyed and dry-lipped,

the saddest song i knew
echoing through my headphones
on an endless loop.

for a moment,
time was still.
for a moment,
everything was okay.

— *then it hit me again, all at once.*

i got home,
packed six years
of my life
into a tidy little box,
and buried it
in the depths of my closet
right beside the garbage bag of old clothes
i'd never fit into again.

— *i'll never understand how so much fit in such
  a small space.*

how am i supposed to go on
pretending everything's okay
when my entire world
has been turned
upside down?

— *i can't do this.*

i needed to *try* to find some sense of normalcy.
i needed to *try* to move on.
i needed to *try* to be
the person i've been
pretending to be
for the past
seven years.

so i went out with my friends,
and i swear i tried,
but you called again.
you told me you were going out,
and i knew the answer
before i asked the question,
but i asked anyway.

not even a week after i stepped off that bus,
you'd already moved on
while i dangled from
a fraying thread,
a shred of hope,
the slightest chance
that you'd come back for me.

— *you'd moved on long before this phone call.*

can former lovers
ever truly go back
to being *just friends?*

— i said yes, but i don't think i meant it.

he now stands where i stood,
and you tell him the things
you told me,
while telling me you've learned
from the mistakes you made
with us.

i wonder where this version of you was
when i was struggling to keep
my head above water.
i wonder what it's like
to simply trade one heart
for another.

— *i am more than your prototype romance.*

the box beckoned me,
like a beating heart
hidden beneath the floorboards,
louder, louder,
it called,
taunting me, mocking me,
louder, louder, louder,
until i had no choice
but one:
i ripped it open,
stuffed its insides
into a big black bag,
and left it on the side of the road
for the crows to feast upon.

— *i admit the deed.*

(an homage to edgar allan poe's "the tell-tale heart")

i'm reaching into my skull
and raking my fingernails
across

e v e r y
i   n c h

of my brain
until i've scrubbed you
entirely
from
my mind.

— *eternal sunshine i.*

colors
drained
out
of
my world
      one
            by
      one
            by
      one,
until life
was
but
shades
of
g r a y.

— *pleasantville i.*

i spent seven years
blowing out birthday candles,
setting alarms for 11:11,
and praying for stars
to fall out of the sky
for one more chance
to wish things right
between us.
it was in that eighth year
that i realized
you leaving
was what
i should have been
wishing for
all along.

— so i wished to never see your face again.

please know
i'm not writing these poems
to dig up all the bodies
buried beneath the flower bed

and line them up next to all
the skeletons in the closet.

this is me
cleaning out the attic
filled with all the things i hid away
from prying eyes

so i could maintain some semblance
of a person who had their shit together.

this is me unpacking all the
overstuffed boxes
and sweeping away all the
cobwebs in the corners.

this is me airing out the lingering stench
of all the things i
didn't say
wouldn't say
couldn't say

— *should've said.*

my mistake
was trying to change you
because i couldn't accept you
for who you were.

— *manic pixie.*

your mistake
was telling me you were someone
you knew
you could never be.

— *dream girl.*

if only you were honest with me
from the start.
if only i was honest with myself
from the start.

— *honesty could've saved the both of us from
    so much pain.*

i used to place the blame
for the way those years played out
solely on your shoulders,
but no more.

we were both too young
to truly know
the consequences
of what we were getting into.

maybe my expectations were too high.
maybe i hung on too hard for too long.
maybe i just couldn't accept the fact that
maybe we weren't meant to be after all.

you've done the unforgivable,
but i shouldn't have held you accountable
for the blood on your hands
while ignoring the blood on mine.

— *hindsight.*

to move on
with my life
i had to cut

you

out of it.

— *i'm not sorry.*

i'd always thought that love
was something to be chased,
something i had to be
in relentless pursuit of,

but to chase love
is to chase heartbreak,
and i haven't a heart
left to break.

— *if love wants me, it knows where to find me.*

every day,
i drove to the same lot.
every day,
i parked in the same spot.
every day,
i simply existed.

— that's all i know how to do at this point.

i don't know if there's a god,
but i said a prayer anyway,
for the one i used to be.
before i burned the body,
filled a bottle with its ashes,
and sent it off to sea.

— for the first time in my life, i could finally swim.

i became an expert
at hiding myself
behind masks,
but there wasn't a mask
big enough,
convincing enough,
to hide this.

— so i became someone else instead.

there was no seeing through
this facade.
there were no seams,
no sign of where *it* ended
and *i* began
because this time,
the face i hid behind
was my own.

— *they always miss what's hiding in plain sight.*

i wore my insecurities like a crown,
head held high,
chin toward the sky,
each step delivered
with the same purpose
that kings
are made of.

— fake it 'til you make it.

i told myself
i would never love again.
i told myself
there wasn't anyone else
out there for me
and even if there was,
i told myself
it didn't matter.

— i was wrong, there was, and it did.

the moment it happened
is difficult to pinpoint,
but as if all at once,

she
became
my past

and

you
became
my future.

— *love seems to find one when they least expect it.*

one look into those honest eyes
and i knew i could
tear myself apart before you,
bare every last piece
of this broken soul
and there would be no judgment,
only understanding.

— *like calls to like.*

tell me everything.
take the weight of the world
off your weary shoulders
and let me carry it on mine,
because you've been
burdened by it
for far too long.

— *rest easy.*

little did i know,
while i was off hiding
in parking lots,
you were doing
the very same thing
hundreds of miles away.

— *parked cars, parked hearts.*

how could it be
that your soul and mine
fit together so completely?

— *you fit me better than my own skin.*

we talked
from dawn to dusk,
thousands of messages
traveling between our fingertips
at lightning speed,
and never once
did we run out of things
to say.

— *i travel light-years in keystrokes.*

you understand me
better than
anyone else
ever has.

you understand me
better than i
understand
myself.

— *one heart, one mind.*

dropkick this broken heart
and make it feel again.

— *DROPKICKromance.*

every lost color returned,

one
         by
one
         by
one

like cherry blossoms

b u r s t i n g
t   o   l   i   f   e

in the spring,
brighter
and more vivid
than ever
before.

— *pleasantville ii.*

you found a bottle
filled with the ashes
of who i used to be
drifting through the wreckage
of a ghost ship.
with a mermaid's kiss,
you filled those ashes
with new life
and me
with new purpose.

— *the phoenix.*

there was just
something about you.
without a word,
you managed to
piece together
what had been
meticulously
picked apart and
put on display
for all to see.

without a word,
you showed me
a heart that knew
what it was like
to have its trust
s h a t t e r e d,
a heart without
the capability of
doing the same
to another.

— *i knew i could trust you from the moment i met you.*

we were broken shards
of stained glass mirrors,
a jagged mess of every color
in the universe.

they shaped us,
shattered us,
and left us
to pick up the pieces.

and so
we pieced each other
back together,

your pieces
mixed with mine,
and mine
mixed with yours.

— *from the broken, we'll make art.*

cutting through the atmosphere
my icy exterior
ignited into a blaze of
stardust.
i hurtled toward the ground
with earth-shattering force
and after long last,
i had something worth
falling for.

— i couldn't have fallen harder or faster.

too many times,
i've allowed
door number two
to slam shut in my face
because i was too busy
propping open

door number one

but this time,
i took off for
door number two
like a plane down a runway
and when i heard the sound of

door number one

slamming shut
behind me,
i didn't
even
flinch.

— *the open door.*

we found each other
in darkness
and made our own light.
together, we burned
brighter than anything
that awaited us
on the other side.

— *the sun has nothing on you.*

when i was lost,
you found me
and took me in.

you gave me love,
you gave me attention,
and you gave me
a home.

— *a stray no longer.*

you bought me a copy
of your favorite book, and
i ate each word like candy—
i devoured chapter after chapter
and when i reached the end
i was left hungry
for more.

reading became
my favorite pastime—

with every turn of the page,
every new chapter,
i got to fall in love
with the same words,
the same characters,
the same places,
that you fell in love with.

— *and it was like falling in love with you all over again.*

in every book i read,
i see you.

i see you
in every heroine
who isn't afraid
to stand up and say whatever's on her mind.

i see you
in every heroine
who wears the term "unlikable"
like a badge of honor.

i see you
in every heroine
who's had to endure the unimaginable
yet still finds the strength to fight another day.

i see you
in every heroine
who's had to carry a revolution
she never asked to be part of in the first place.

— *you are the strongest person i know.*

                                        she
                              c r e p t
                    back
              into
        my
life

like i was another one
of the bad habits
she just couldn't quit,

but i was no longer dependent
on her high to get by.
she *was* my bad habit
but i now have the strength to quit.

— i was never one for self-destruction.

i gave her one chance
to prove to me
that we really could be friends
after all we'd been through,
but soon enough,
her intentions were all too clear.

— *there is no sequel to this story.*

she tried to break
what we built,
but she couldn't even
scratch the surface.

— her last stand was her final fall.

did you honestly think
i'd sit around
and wait for you
forever?

— *i've wasted enough of my life on you.*

if it's my forgiveness you want,
i will give it.

i forgive you
for making me enjoy
the taste
of poison.

i forgive you
for sowing seeds in my soul
that birthed my
demons and ghosts.

i forgive you
knowing we are two
very different people now
than we were then.

but i cannot forgive you
for setting fire
to the home that now
houses my heart

when you couldn't accept
that i'd finally learned
to live and love
without you.

and i cannot forgive you
for thinking so little of the love that
theprincessturneddamselturnedqueen
and i had forged despite you

that you thought i would
come crawling back to you
the second you decided to
come crawling back to me.

this is where
we stand.
this is where
we end.

— *i have forgiven; now let me forget.*

so tear up the photos.
burn the letters.
scrub my name from your wall,
and my fingerprints from your heart.
delete my phone number,
wipe me from
your memory,
and forget
i ever
e x i s t e d.

— *eternal sunshine ii.*

blowing up bridges
    is always better
        when someone else is
            pushing the button
                with you.

— explosions make for great first dates.

hand in hand,
we exorcised
our demons.

hand in hand,
we'll ward off
our ghosts.

— *there isn't anything we can't overcome.*

we had the makings
of star-crossed lovers,
but we fought our way
across solar systems,
leaving new planets
in our wake
as the pull of
our shooting-star hearts
formed a galaxy
all their own.

— *big bang theory.*

i've wasted so many
years of my life
on a journey
to find
myself

but that journey finally
came to an end
when i first
looked into
your eyes.

— *twin souls.*

what is more innocent
than a girl and her cat?

— *her shadow.*

your sister and i sat in the kitchen
as you brewed a pot of coffee.
when you filled my mug,
you did it the very same way

you filled my heart:

completely oblivious
to just how vital
either would become
to my everyday life.

— *i savor every drop.*

you and me,
the sun peeking through
the flame-topped trees,
windows cracked,
that song about
autumn gold
filling the calm
around us.

you and me,
fingers laced,
your hand
squeezing gently
like a pulse,
a sign that we
couldn't be more alive
than we are in this moment.

— *like leaves, we are falling.*

we packed a picnic
and you whisked me away
to your favorite place,

where we ate sandwiches
on everything bagels,
drank pumpkin spice coffee,

took pictures with our faces
hidden behind our favorite book,
and got lost in each other.

— you are my favorite place.

i picked up
the single red leaf
lying atop the
hueless remains
of those that had
fallen before it,
and held it up to the sky

like a flickering flame
against a tidal wave,
i looked at you and said
"i have yet to find
a single thing
as vibrant
as you."

— *autumn has nothing on you.*

in the spring,
you showed me
what it was
to live.

— *vernal equinox.*

in the autumn,
you showed me
what it was
to be alive.

— *autumnal equinox.*

october:
birth and rebirth,
steaming cups of coffee,
treetops igniting above us
like newly stricken matchsticks.
"just like your hair," you'd say.

you called me
your "october boy"
and i became determined,
now more than ever before,
to be someone worthy
of your love.

— *october soul mates.*

the ghosts of my past
refuse to stop haunting me.
they snake into my skull
and wrap their inky tendrils
around my mind.

they tell me
i don't deserve this.
they tell me
she'll find someone better.
they tell me

this
cannot
last.

— *and i don't know how to tell them they're wrong.*

there are some wounds
that love cannot heal.
some scars are just too deep,
and all you can do is hope
that time really
does what it promised.

i fear i am too far gone,
too broken,
that no amount of time
will undo
what has been done
to me.

— i'm sorry; you don't deserve this.

i will weave you
a wreath of fallen leaves
and place it upon your head
like a crown of golden flames,
for you are a queen
and from the autumn ashes,
you reign supreme.

— *your most obedient servant.*

i placed my heart in your palm
wrapped your fingers around it
the way i wrapped my scarf
around your neck
when you said it was too cold,
and kissed the back
of your hand.

a promise
that this was only temporary,
a promise
that i would be back;
a promise
that no matter what,
i am yours.

— *this is not goodbye.*

i've never been good
at parting ways—
i often cry too hard
too early
for too long,
leaving pillowcases damp
and highways streaked
with salt-stained regret.

— *separation anxiety.*

i sat in terminal b
of newark international
hiding tears behind
sunglasses.

leaving you
was the last thing
i ever wanted
to do,

but gorgeous,
i swear to you
i'll be back
before you know it.

— *ewr* ➠ *dtw*

the only thing i could do
to fill the void
the distance left me with
was to cling to the clothes
that still carried your scent,
and take my coffee
the same way you take yours.

— *i think it made me miss you more.*

i could see your face
and hear your voice
but now that i've
known your touch,
there's no living
without it.

— *if only i could reach through this screen.*

i look out
the backseat window
of the car filled
with all of my
best friends
and rest my eyes
on the moon,
and i wonder:

how can it be
that the moon is surrounded
by all of the stars
in the nighttime sky
and yet
it still looks so isolated
from the rest of the universe
around it?

— *lonely ≠ alone.*

time
is the
achilles' heel
of distance.
with enough of it,
no distance
is too great
to overcome.

— *i'm coming home to you.*

we crashed into each other's arms
as if another second apart
would've killed us,
and it was then i made
a silent vow;
a promise
to never let the miles
stand between us
again.

— *our greatest triumph.*

waking up early
just to stop by
your house and see you
for the few moments it took us
to have a cup of
morning coffee
together.

— *i want every second of you i can get.*

if this was truly
meant to be,
i had to earn the trust of
the two most
important people
in your life:

your dad
and
your cat.

— *thankfully, both approved.*

morning coffee turned into
after-work coffee,
turned into
before-bed coffee,
turned into
a mug in your cupboard
a toothbrush in your bathroom
and three totes full of my belongings
in the spare bedroom.

— *a natural progression.*

i could spend eternity
following you around
every corner
of every bookstore
watching you search for
the perfect story
to get lost in.

— *your passion is my passion.*

before we flew to michigan,
i had to get your father's approval.
my stomach twisted itself into knots
and i could hear the screams
of every single nerve in my body.

he had already accepted me into his home
and treated me like a member of his family
but there was so much riding on
this one question,
i just couldn't take the thought of hearing *no.*

i caught him in the hallway,
showed him the
tiny amethyst heart
inside the little black box
as my own heart
slammed against my ribcage.

two seconds felt like
two lifetimes,
but with a smile,
a handshake,
and a wish of good luck,

the only thing left to do
was make it official.

— thank you for accepting me with open arms.

i carved out the center
of our favorite book
and buried my heart
inside of it.

i led you to
the wooden fairytale bridge
overlooking the river
and dropped to a knee.

looking into your eyes
i opened to the bookmarked page
and asked the most important question
that would ever pass through these lips.

— 08/25/15.

let's build
bookshelves together
and fill them
with our story.

— *ours will always be my favorite.*

knowing that you're
willing to share
the rest of your life
with me

is knowing that
there must be
some good
inside of me.

— *somewhere.*

you gave me books
and showed me
how to live
a thousand and one lives.

you gave me a pen
and showed me
how to write
this one.

— i owe my voice to you.

crack open
my skull, pour
me out, and
take what you
need.

everything
i am
everything
i've been
everything
i ever will be

is yours.

— *i just can't seem to make it all come out right.*

it's easy
to turn the hurt
into poetry.

hurt is ugly—
it doesn't need
to be wrapped in a bow
or buried beneath a bed of roses.

turning the good
into poetry
is much more difficult.

capturing the way
you glance at me out of the corner of your eye
when you know i'm gazing at you
as if seeing an autumn sunset
for the first time—

or the way
your legs get tangled with mine underneath the table
at our favorite coffee shop
as we spill our hearts
into word documents—

or how
our pinkies interlocking as we walk in the park
has more meaning
than if we reached into the sky
and wrote our names amongst stars.

no, turning the good
into poetry
is much more difficult,

because these moments
are already poetic,
and putting them into words

is like translating
from one language
to another,
and something always
gets lost in translation.

— *you are living, breathing poetry.*

you believed in me
when i didn't believe
in myself.
you taught me
how to love again
when i had lost
all hope.
you showed me how
to be a person
i could finally
be proud of.
if not for you,
i would not be the person
i am today.
if not for you,
i would not be.

— *for that, i thank you.*

in saving yourself,
you saved me.

— *the princess saves him in this one.*

acknowledgments

this book would not have been possible without the many who've supported me along this journey.

thank you to my family: my mother, maria, for always believing that i could achieve whatever i set my mind on. my nonna, rita, for being the most kindhearted individual i have ever known. my brother and tag team partner, jon, and sister-in-law, victoria, for always being there for amanda and me and for always rolling out the red carpet for us whenever we come back to michigan. and my sister, sarah, for being the model of what a fighter is.

to my in-laws, terry, sue, courtney, aj, and the kids: thank you for treating me like a part of your family from day one—i couldn't have asked for a better one to marry into.

to professor evans: thank you for helping build my confidence as a writer from the ground up and for helping me rediscover my love of writing (and edgar allan poe) when i wasn't so sure this path was for me. your guidance and support continue to impact me. i am so very lucky to have been your student.

to professor lineberry: because of you, i keep a journal on me at all times, i try to freewrite every day, and i know that poetry doesn't need to follow any sort of rules. thank you for your teachings and for your support and encouragement.

to trista, christine, danika, shauna, mira, and megan: *DROPKICKromance* wouldn't be what it is without you. your feedback and willingness to give it to me straight were integral in taking this collection to the next level, and words cannot begin to express my gratitude for all your help.

to islam farid: thank you for giving me the perfect cover to slap on the front of my first book. they say not to judge a book by its cover, but i know people do, and i'm thankful i have a cover that will put more eyes on my work.

to j.r. rogue and kat savage, who came up with the prompt that inspired the poem "*and it tears in two*": you two are some of the best poets out there today, and i sincerely hope you find every bit of success that you two are working so hard for. thank you for being such inspirations.

to all the modern-day women poets that came before me: thank you for revitalizing the poetry scene and making poetry accessible to the masses. you paved the way for people like me to put our work out there, and every time i write a poem, i do so knowing who made it possible.

to my editor, patty rice: the day you emailed me and told me you had my book proposal is one i will not soon forget. thank you for believing in me and my words and for all the work you've put into not only *DROPKICKromance* but also the entirety of the modern-day poetry scene.

to the rest of the andrews mcmeel team: to be a part of the amp family is honestly a dream come true. thank you for seeing enough potential in my work to take the risk of putting it out in the world. this has been nothing short of an honor.

to all of my friends, as well as the online poetry community: there are so many of you who have supported me in all sorts of different ways, and i appreciate each and every single one of you more than you know. i'd name names, but i fear i'd forget someone important, and that's the last thing i want to do. thank you for being the greatest support system anybody could ever hope for.

to amanda: this book would not exist without you. i would not exist without you. thank you for your unconditional love and support. thank you for letting me bounce ideas off you incessantly and for giving me your honest feedback. most importantly, thank you for being you.

and last but certainly not least, to you, the reader: thank you. thank you for giving me and this book a chance. thank you for coming on this journey with me. this story is not over—it's only just begun. right now, i am relacing my boots and readjusting my aim, and i hope you'll continue to stand by my side as i take on the world, one dropkick at a time.

— *cyrus parker.*

about the author

cyrus parker is a pro-wrestler-turned-poet, hailing from a small town in new jersey, where he lives with his poetess wife, amanda lovelace. originally from michigan, where he spent half a decade working on the local independent wrestling scene, cyrus is now trading his literal dropkicks for literary dropkicks as he puts wrestling on the back burner to pursue his other passion, writing.

a creative writing major at brookdale community college in lincroft, nj, the self-proclaimed DROPKICKpoet has set out on a journey to find his voice, and himself, through the written word. when he's not illegibly scrawling away in his journal or typing away on his next project, cyrus can be found napping excessively after consuming massive amounts of coffee or wandering the world, trying to be the very best pokémon master who ever lived.

DROPKICKromance is cyrus's debut poetry collection and the first book in the *DROPKICKpoetry* series.

WEBSITE: http://cyrusparker.com
TWITTER: @cyrusparker
INSTAGRAM: @cyrusparker

index

INDEX

index

INDEX

index

DROPKICK*romance*

Andrews McMeel Publishing
a division of Andrews McMeel Universal
1130 Walnut Street, Kansas City, Missouri 64106

www.andrewsmcmeel.com

18 19 20 21 22 BVG 10 9 8 7 6 5 4 3 2 1

ISBN: 978-1-4494-9300-4

Library of Congress Control Number: 2017952480

Editor: Patty Rice
Art Director/Designer: Diane Marsh
Production Editor: Elizabeth A. Garcia
Production Manager: Cliff Koehler

Cover design by Islam Farid
www.islamfarid.net

ATTENTION: SCHOOLS AND BUSINESSES

Andrews McMeel books are available at quantity discounts with
bulk purchase for educational, business, or sales promotional use.
For information, please e-mail the Andrews McMeel Publishing
Special Sales Department: specialsales@amuniversal.com.